# Watch It Grow
# Duck
## Barrie Watts

W
## FRANKLIN WATTS
LONDON • SYDNEY

This edition 2005

First published in 2002 by Franklin Watts
96 Leonard Street, London EC2A 4XD

Franklin Watts Australia
45-51 Huntley Street, Alexandria, NSW 2015

© Barrie Watts 2002


Editor: Adrian Cole
Art director: Jonathan Hair
Photographer: Barrie Watts
Illustrator: David Burroughs
Consultant: Beverley Mathias, REACH

A CIP catalogue record for this book
is available from the British Library


ISBN 0 7496 6119 4

Dewey Classification 594

Printed in Hong Kong, China

## How to use this book

Watch It Grow has been specially designed to cater for a range of reading and learning abilities. Initially children may just follow the pictures. Ask them to describe in their own words what they see. Other children will enjoy reading the single sentence in large type, in conjunction with the pictures. This single sentence is then expanded in the main text. More adept readers will be able to follow the text and pictures by themselves through to the conclusion of the life cycle.

# Contents

# Ducks come from eggs.

Here is a white duck egg at its actual size. It is about the same size as a large chicken egg.

Duck eggs have a hard shell and are filled with **yolk** and white.

During the spring, a female duck can lay around 15 eggs in her nest.

She uses feathers from her body to line the nest. Next, the duck **incubates** the eggs. The warmth of her body helps a tiny duckling grow inside each egg.

# The egg hatches.

After 28 days, the duckling begins to hatch out of the egg. It uses the hard tip of its bill to break the tough skin that covers the inside of the shell.

Slowly the egg cracks and
pieces of shell fall away.
The duckling can breathe air
for the first time in its life.

# The duckling breaks out.

It takes up to 48 hours for the duckling to break out of the egg completely. It is tired and its feathers are wet. The duckling's mother keeps it warm until its feathers dry out.

The duckling still has some
of the egg **yolk** in its body.
Over the next few days it will use
the yolk for food, until it is strong
enough to find something to eat.

# The feathers are dry.

Two hours after hatching the duckling is dry. Its fluffy feathers are called **down**. The down keeps the duckling warm, but it is not **waterproof**.

If the duckling
gets cold and
wet it could die,
so it stays safe
in the nest.
The duckling
sleeps and rests
in the nest for
about four days.

# The duckling gets stronger.

After four days, the duckling's legs are strong enough for it to walk without falling over.
It has used up all the **yolk** in its body and is very hungry.

The duckling flaps its stumpy wings to make them stronger. But it will have to wait until it grows its adult feathers before it can fly.

# The duckling swims.

The duckling takes its first
swim with its mother. It stays
very close to her. The duckling
loves being in the water.

It will spend longer each day swimming, feeding and washing itself. Even though it can swim easily with its **webbed feet**, the duckling at this age cannot stay in the cold water for too long. Its **down** will get too wet.

# The duckling feeds.

The duckling eats water weeds and other plants. As it swims it also looks for food under the water. Its eyes are protected by a thin layer of skin.

The duckling also eats seeds and anything else that looks like food.

If it eats something **inedible**, like a twig, the duckling spits it out.
The duckling needs to eat a lot every day to keep growing and stay healthy.

# The duckling goes for a walk.

The duckling also looks for food on land. It eats grass and crawling insects.

The duckling's legs are stronger, but
it still needs to rest during the day.
It usually returns to the water when it
is tired. It is safer there than on land
where it might be eaten by **predators**.

# The duckling cleans itself.

The duckling washes by
splashing water over its
body. As soon as it
comes out of the water,
it **preens** itself.

It checks the fluffy **down**
with its bill to make sure
that it is clean.
The down must be kept
in good condition to keep
the duckling warm.

# The duckling's bill changes.

After three weeks, the duckling's bill has doubled in size. The bill is made from a tough material, similar to that of human fingernails.

The bill hardens and changes colour as the duckling grows older. Inside the bill are tiny, soft teeth. These help the duckling to grip slippery water weeds and tear tough grass.

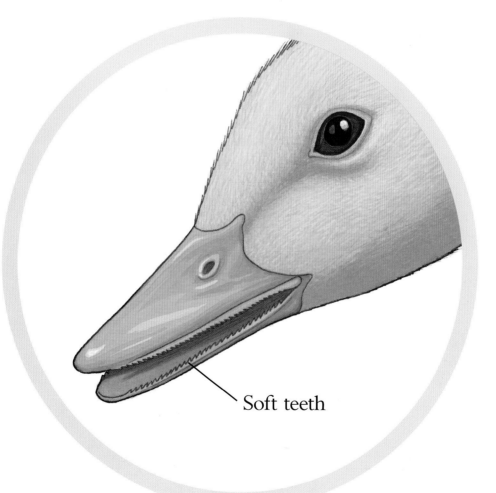

Soft teeth

# The adult feathers grow.

When it is a month old, the duckling starts to grow its white adult feathers. They are made of a material called **keratin**. They push out some of the fluffy **down**.

The **down** closest to the duckling's body is not pushed out. It remains and helps the duckling to stay warm.

As the duckling grows older, it will shed its feathers several times. This is called **moulting**.

The duck flaps its wings.

Three months after hatching, the duck is almost fully grown. Soon it will be able to fly. However, its wing muscles are not strong enough yet.

The duck flaps its wings to exercise the muscles and make them stronger.

Throughout the winter ducks live together. They feed and try to survive the cold weather.

# The adult ducks mate.

The following spring, the adult duck looks for a partner with whom to mate. After mating, the female duck makes a nest from dried grass, leaves and fluffy **down**.

She lays her eggs in the nest
and then **incubates** them.
Four weeks later ducklings
will hatch out.

# Word bank

**Down** - the soft, fluffy feathers that cover the body of a duckling and keep it warm. Even when a duckling gets adult feathers it will still keep some of its down.

**Incubate** - when a bird sits on its eggs to keep them warm so they will hatch.

**Inedible** - something that cannot be eaten, such as a twig or stone.

**Keratin** - the material from which feathers are made. It is flexible and light in weight.

**Moulting** - when a bird sheds its feathers.

**Predator** - an animal that hunts and eats another animal. A fox is a duck's main predator.

**Preen** - when a bird cleans its feathers with its bill to keep them healthy and tidy.

**Waterproof** - when water cannot pass through something. The down of a duckling is not waterproof.

**Webbed feet** - these feet have toes that are joined together by thin pieces of skin.

**Yolk** - the food in an egg that is eaten by a duckling when it is very young.

# Life cycle

After 28 days the duckling uses its bill to tap through the shell of its egg.

Next spring, after mating, the female duck lays its own eggs.

The duckling breaks out. It is tired and wet.

After three months the duck is almost fully grown.

After four days the duckling can walk and swim.

One month after hatching the duckling grows adult feathers.

The duckling looks for crawling insects to eat.

After three weeks the duckling's bill is larger and stronger.

# Index